Name

Flip Fun!

Choose your favorite letter. Draw five things which begin with that letter.

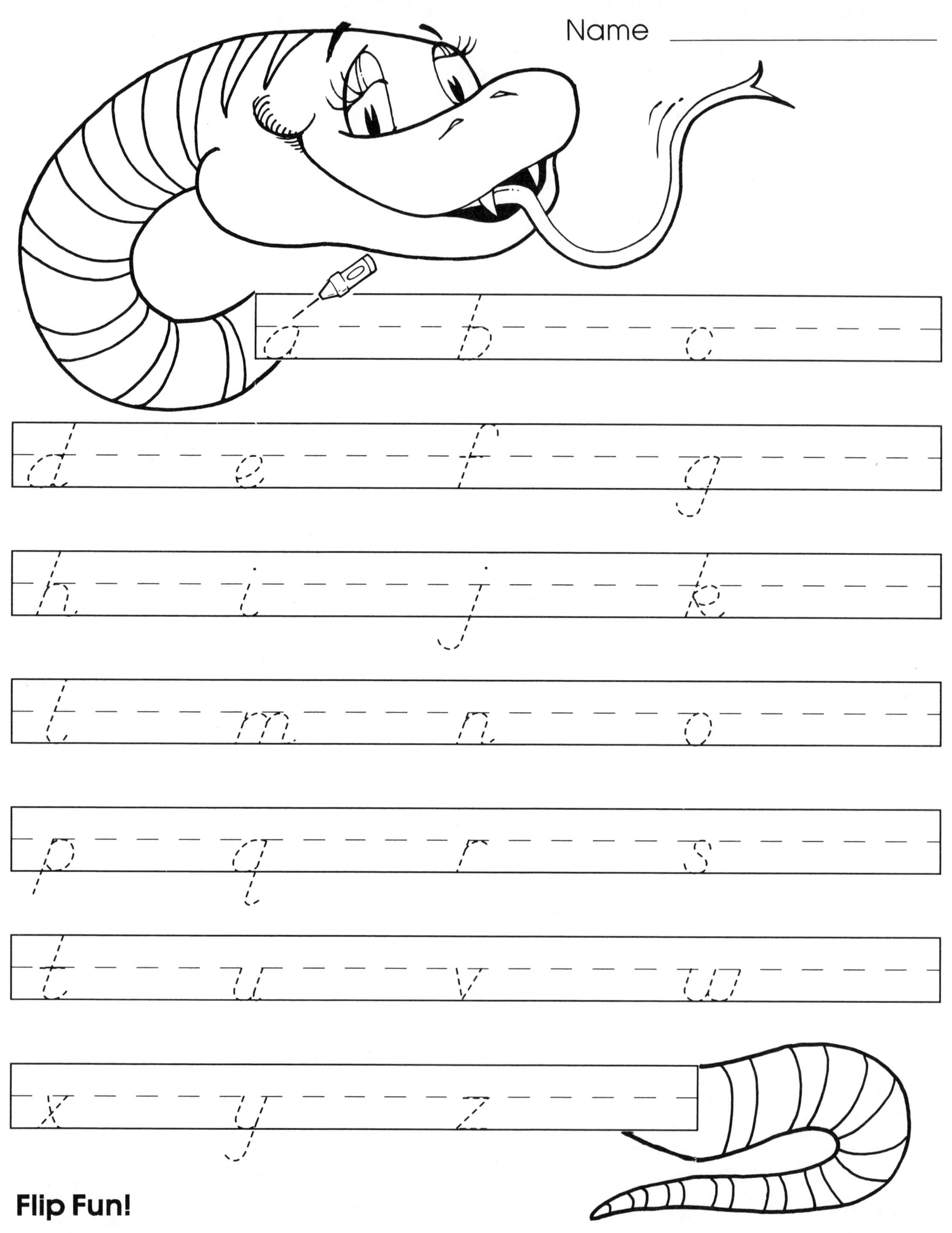

Flip Fun!

Choose the letter which begins your first name. Draw five things which begin with that letter.

Name ____________________

Flip Fun!

Draw an animal that begins with A and an animal that begins with Z.

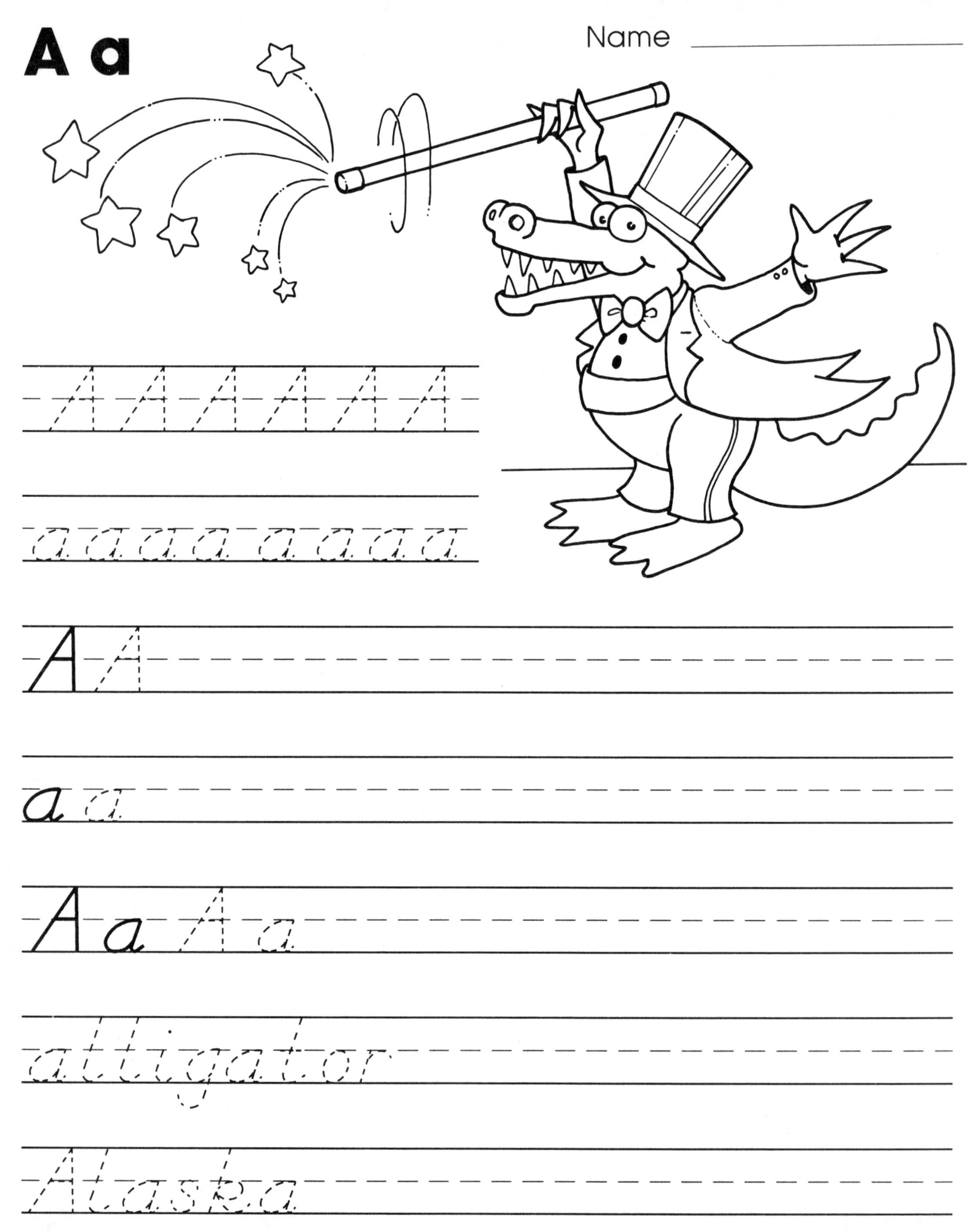

Flip Fun!

Draw three things that begin with A.

A a

Name ______________

A A

a a

Anna

away

Ants are apple artists.

Flip Fun!

Draw a tree with 3 red apples and 3 green apples.

Name ____________________

Aa

Ants adjust accordians.

Alligators are acrobats.

Flip Fun!

Draw an alligator eating an apricot.

B b

Name ______________________

Flip Fun!

Draw a bunny holding a red, a blue, a yellow and a green balloon.

B b

Name ____________________

B

b

Bobby

bubbles

Baby bears bite bananas.

Flip Fun!

Draw a teddy bear eating another food that begins with B.

Name ______________________

Bb

Bzzzzzzzzzzz

Bzzzzzzzz

Bees buzz by bridges.

BUG

Bugs blow brass bugles.

BaN

Flip Fun!

Draw a bat taking a bubble bath. Color the bubbles blue.

C c

Name ________________

Flip Fun!

Draw five fluffy yellow clouds. Put a big blue C on each one.

Cc

Name ____________

C c

c c

Calvin

candy

Clumsy cooks carry cakes.

Flip Fun!

Draw a big yellow cake. Put blue candles on it to show how old you are.

Name ___________________

Clowns catch candy.

Chimps cut coconuts.

Flip Fun!

Draw a colorful clown.

D d

Name ____________________

Flip Fun!

Draw a big green dragon and two more animals that begin with D.

D d

Name ________________

D D

d d

David

did

Damp ducks dance.

Flip Fun!

Draw five purple dishes. Put a brown donut on each dish.

Name

D d

Ducks decorate donuts.

Dolphins direct divers.

Flip Fun!

Draw a dinosaur dunking a donut.

E e

Name ______________________

E E elf eight

e e eleven

E e E e

elephant

Earth

Flip Fun!

Draw eight envelopes. Put a green E on each one.

E e

Name ____________

E E

e e

Ernie

every

Elves eat eight eggs.

Flip Fun!

Draw an Easter basket. Put eight colorful eggs in the basket.

Name ______________________

Energetic eels exercise.

Elephants exit elevators.

Flip Fun!

Draw an eel going down an escalator.

F f

Name ____________________

F F F F F F

f f f f f f f f

F F

f f

F f F f

fish

Florida

Flip Fun!

Draw five orange fish in a big black frying pan.

F f

Name ________________

F F

f f

Fred

fifth

Four fat foxes feast.

Flip Fun!

Draw five things you would find on a farm.

Name ______________________

Ff

Five fairies fix fudge.

Frogs fry French fries.

Flip Fun!

Draw a fruit you like to eat. Color it.

G g

Name ________________

G G G G G G

g g g g g g g g

G G

g g

Gg Gg

ghost

Georgia

Flip Fun! Draw a ghost blowing a big bubble with his gum. Put a purple G on the gum.

G g

Name ____________________

G

g

George

giggle

Gorillas give great gifts.

Flip Fun!

Draw four green gifts that begin with G.

Name ______________________

Gg

Grasshoppers giggle.

Geese gobble grapes.

Flip Fun!

Draw a gingerbread house and a garden.

H h

Name ______________________

H H H H H H H H H H H

h h h h h h h h

H H

h h

H h H h

hamburger

Hawaii

Flip Fun!

Draw a plate with two hamburgers and two hot dogs on it.

H h

Name ____________________

H

h

Harry

honey

Horse hotels have hay.

Flip Fun!

Draw a big brown horse wearing a yellow hat with a red heart on it.

Name ______________________

Hh

Hippos have huge hats.

Hogs hike high hills.

Flip Fun!

Draw a helicopter.

I i

Name ________________________

Flip Fun! Draw an ice cream cone with a yellow, a green, a purple and an orange scoop.

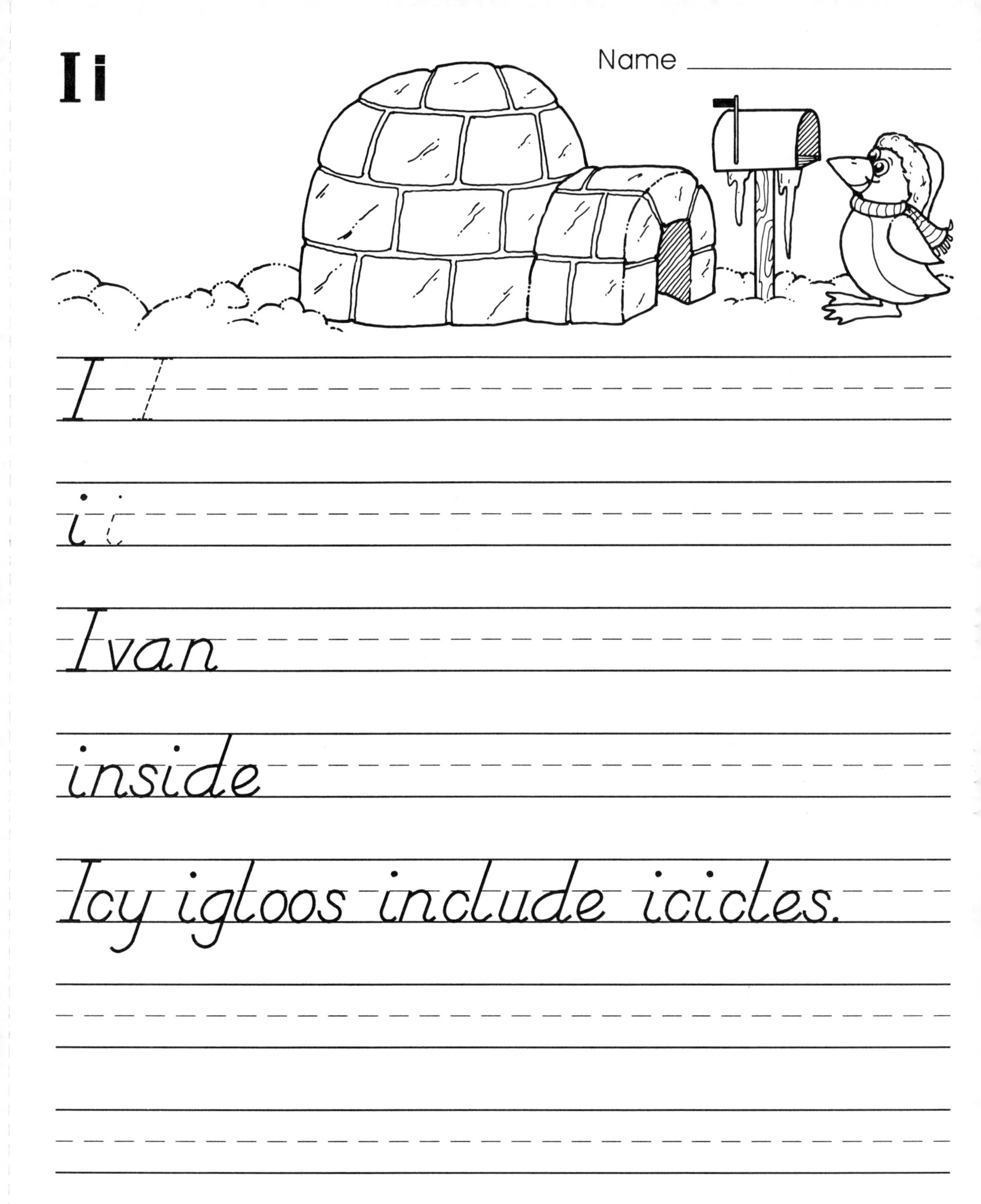

Flip Fun!

Draw the inside of an igloo.

Name ______________________

Ii

Iguanas ink initials.

Inchworms ice icicles.

Flip Fun!

Draw an island. Draw an ice-cream stand on it.

J j

Name ____________________

Flip Fun! Draw three jets flying in a row. Color the first one green, the middle one orange and the last one purple.

J j

Name ________________

J J

j j

John

juice

Jellybeans juggle jacks.

Flip Fun!

Draw a jar filled with colorful jellybeans.

Name

Jj

Jellyfish juggle jars.

Jittery joggers jump.

Flip Fun!

Draw four things you can juggle. Color each one a different color.

K k

Name ____________________

K K K K K K K

k k k k k k k k

K K

k k

K k K k

key

Kentucky

Flip Fun! Draw a key ring. Put a red, a blue, a yellow, a green, a purple and an orange key on the ring.

K k

Name ____________________

K

k

Kim

kick

Kind king kisses kitten.

Flip Fun!

Draw a kitten flying a purple, a green and an orange kite.

Name ______________

Kk

Koalas kindle kindness.

Kangaroos kiss kittens.

Flip Fun!

Draw two knee socks. Color one red and one purple.

L l

Name ________________

L l

L l L l

lamb

Lassie

Flip Fun!

Draw ten leaves. Color five green and five orange.

L l

Name ______________________

L

l

Linda

lilac

Ladybugs lick lollipops.

Flip Fun!

Draw six lollipops. Color two purple, two yellow and two red.

Name ______________________

Llamas lock lockers.

Lobsters like lemonade.

Flip Fun!

Draw five ladders. Color two blue, two yellow and one orange.

M m

Name ____________________

M M M M M

m m m m m m

M M

m m

M m M m

moon

Mars

Flip Fun!

Draw a picture of yourself on the moon.

M m

Name ______________________

M M

m m

Mary

mushroom

Mice make mud pies.

Flip Fun!

Draw five brown mud pies. Put a big red M on each one.

Name ________________

Mm

Mary made meatballs.

Moose mix malts.

Flip Fun!

Draw a mask you would like to wear. Color it.

N n

Name ______________

N N N N N N N N

n n n n n n n n n

N N

n n

Nn Nn

nest

Neptune

Flip Fun! Draw a brown nest with four redbirds in it.
Draw a brown nest with three bluebirds in it.

N n

Name ______________

N N

n n

Nan

noon

Nurses need needles.

Flip Fun!

Draw five pictures that begin with the sound of N.

Name ____________________

Nn

Nancy needs notes.

Newts nail numbers.

Flip Fun!

Draw three things you like to nibble.

O o

Name ____________________

Flip Fun!

Draw a picture to show an octopus living in the ocean.

O o

Name

O O

o o

Oscar

ocean

Owls order oval olives.

Flip Fun!

Draw four things with an oval shape.

Name ____________________

O o

Ollie opens oatmeal.

Oysters oil old oars.

Flip Fun!

Draw five things that can be orange.

P p

Name ______________________

P P P P P P P

p p p p p p p p

P P

p p

P p P p

pizza

Pluto

Flip Fun!

Draw a big pizza divided into four pieces. Put a purple P on each piece.

P p

Name ______________________

P P

p p

Patty

people

Pigs plan perfect picnics.

Flip Fun! Draw a big brown picnic basket.
Draw the food you would pack for a perfect picnic.

Name ______________________

Pp

Penguins park pickups.

Pigs pop popcorn.

Flip Fun!

Draw ten puffy pillows. Draw three polka dots on each one.

Q q

Name ____________________

Q Q Q Q Q Q

q q q q q q q q

Q Q

q q

Q q Q q

quarter

Quebec

Flip Fun!

Draw eight quarters. Draw what you would buy with eight quarters.

Q q

Name ____________________

Q Q

q q

Quincy

quart

Queens quilt quickly.

Flip Fun!

Draw three things you do quietly.

Name ______________________

Qq

Quail quiver quietly.

Queens quilt.

Flip Fun!

Draw five things you can do quickly.

Flip Fun!

Draw where you would like to go in space and what you would see.

R r

Name ____________________

FINISH

R R

r r

Robert

river

Rabbits run races rapidly.

Flip Fun!

Draw ten fluffy rabbits' tails. Put a big red R on each one.

Name ____________

Rr

Rats read recipes.

Robots rent rabbits.

Flip Fun!

Draw a robot and you doing something together.

S s

Name ________________

S S S S S S

s s s s s s s s

S S

s s

Ss Ss

seal

Saturn

Flip Fun! Draw a seal playing with six balls. Color two balls red, two balls green and two balls blue.

S s

Name ____________

S S

s s

Sarah

season

Swans sip sweet sodas.

Flip Fun!

Draw seven sodas with seven straws.

Name ______________________

Ss

Starfish serve supper.

Seals scrub subs.

Flip Fun!

Draw seven things that make you smile.

Tt

Name ____________

Flip Fun!

Draw a big TV. Draw your favorite program on the TV.

T t

Name ____________

T

t

Tina

taste

Two toads tap-dance.

Flip Fun!

Draw a turtle talking on a telephone.

Name

Tt

Turkeys teeter-totter.

Turtles taste tacos.

Flip Fun!

Draw ten things that taste good.

U u

Name ______________________

Flip Fun!

Draw what you like to do on a rainy day.

Flip Fun!

Draw a place where you think unicorns might live.

Name ______________

Uu

Umpires use umbrellas.

Unicorns undo urns.

Flip Fun!

Draw four things that can be found under the sea.

Flip Fun! Draw a green vase filled with ten purple violets. Put a purple V on the vase.

V v

Name ______________________

V V

v v

Vana

vegetable

Vultures visit vampires.

Flip Fun!

Draw three things that begin with V.

Name ___________________

V v

Vultures view violets.

Vampires vacuum.

Flip Fun!

Draw a place you would like to go on vacation.

Flip Fun! Draw a big red watermelon with ten black seeds.
Draw a little red watermelon with five black seeds.

W w

Name ____________________

W W

w w

Wally

window

Worms wiggle wildly.

Flip Fun!

Draw five brown worms in a swimming pool.

Name ______________

W w

Willy wants water.

Wasps wear wigs.

Flip Fun!

Draw a picture of your favorite wig.

X x

Name ________________

Flip Fun!

Draw how you might look in an x-ray.

X x

Name ____________________

X X

x x

Xavier

x-ray

X-man x-rays xylophones.

Flip Fun!

Draw three more musical instruments.

Name ______________________

Xx

Xina x-rayed x-rays.

Xylophones Xerox x's.

Flip Fun!

Draw a treasure map. Put a big X where the treasure is buried.

Y y

Name ______________________

Y Y Y Y Y Y

y y y y y y y y

Y Y

y y

Yy Yy

yo-yo

Yukon

Flip Fun!

Draw six yo-yos. Put a purple Y on each one.

Y y

Name ______________

Y y

y y

Yolanda

yesterday

Yaks yell, "Yummy yams!"

Flip Fun!

Draw a big dish of yummy, yellow yogurt.

Name ____________________

Yy

Yaks yank yo-yos.

Yellow yams yawn.

Flip Fun!

Draw four things you do in your yard.

Z z

Name ______________________

Flip Fun!

Draw five zoo animals.

Z z

Name ____________

Z

z

Zelda

zigzag

Zebras zip zippers.

Flip Fun!

Draw four things you wear that could have zippers on them.

Name ______________________

Z z

Zippers zigzag.

Zany zombies zoom.

Flip Fun!

Draw a design using zigzag lines. Use many different colors.

Name ____________________

Color, trace and write.

Flip Fun!

Draw five pictures with your favorite color.

Name ______________________

Trace and write.

Sunday

Monday

Tuesday

Wednesday

Thursday

Friday

Saturday

Flip Fun!

Choose your favorite day. Draw what you like to do on that day.

Color, trace and write.

Name ______________________

1 one

2 two

3 three

4 four

5 five

Flip Fun!

Draw five colorful kites.

Color, trace and write.

Name ____________________

6 six

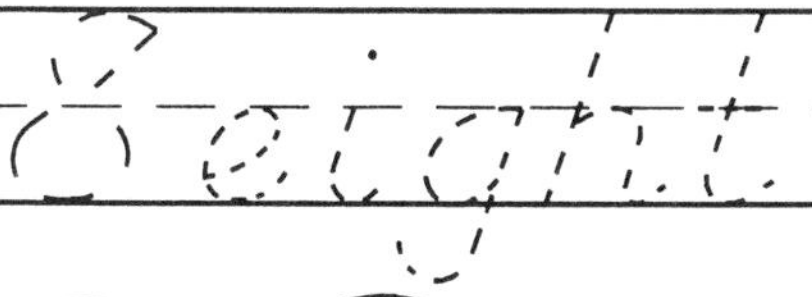

7 seven

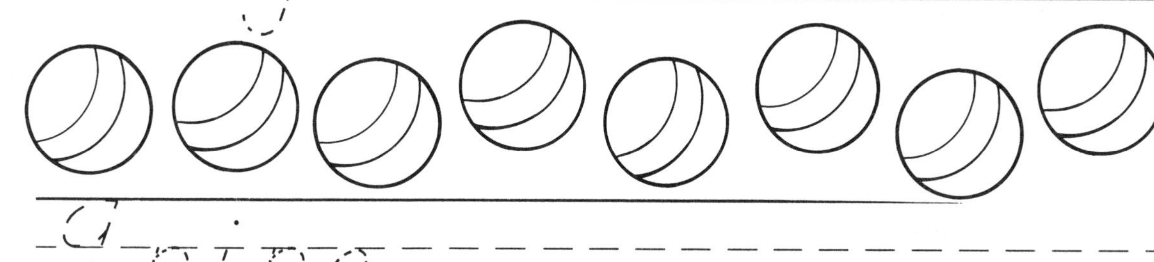

8 eight

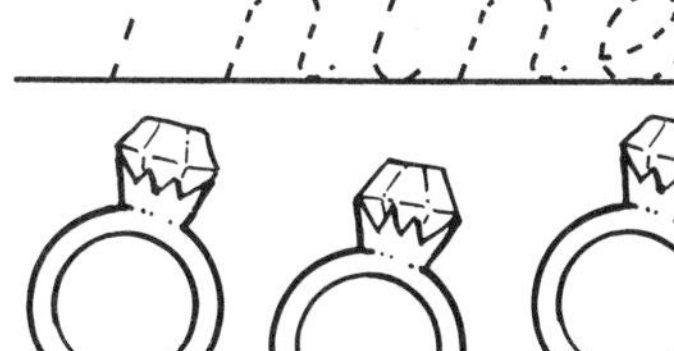

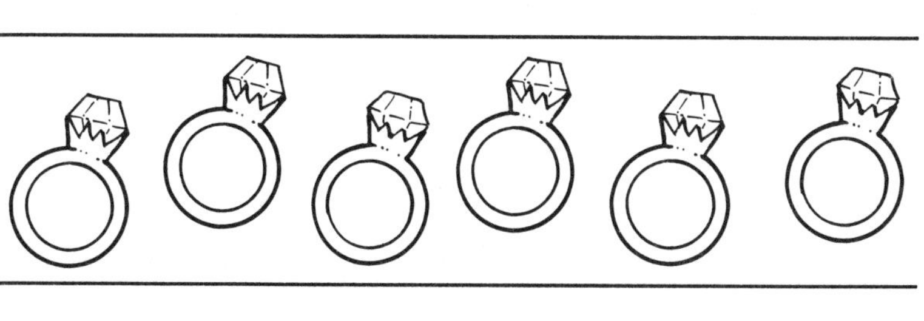

9 nine

10 ten

Flip Fun!

Draw ten colorful butterflies.

Color, trace and write. Name ____________

11

11 eleven

12

12 twelve

13

13 thirteen

14

14 fourteen

15

15 fifteen

Flip Fun! Draw fifteen colorful flowers.

Color, trace and write. Name

16

16 sixteen

17

17 seventeen

18

18 eighteen

19

19 nineteen

20

20 twenty

Flip Fun! Draw twenty colorful balloons.

Merry Months

Name ____________________

Color, trace and write.

January

February

March

April

May

June

Flip Fun!

Draw a picture of what your favorite time of year looks like.

Monthly Medley

Name ____________________

Color, trace and write.

July

August

September

October

November

December

Flip Fun! Choose your favorite month. Draw a picture of what you like to do during the month.

Family Portrait

Name ______________________

Color, trace and write.

Flip Fun! Draw a picture of your family.

Getting into Shapes

Name ____________________

Color, trace and write.

circle

square

triangle

rectangle

diamond

Flip Fun! Draw a picture using only the shapes on this page.

Money in the Bank

Name ______________________

Trace and write.

cents

penny

nickel

dime

quarter

half dollar

dollar

Flip Fun! Draw something you would buy with one dollar.

Where?

Name ______________________

Trace and write.

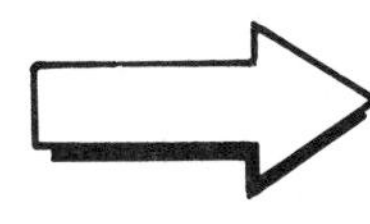

right

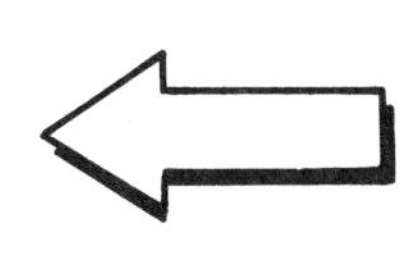

left

up

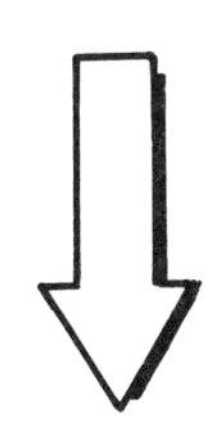

down

over

under

around

Flip Fun! Draw a cat on the left side of the paper. Draw a dog on the right.

School Is Out for the Day

Name ___________________

What do you like to do after school?
Trace and finish each sentence.

After School Activities

play alone	play with friends	play with pets
climb a tree	swing on a swing	read a book
jump rope	play ball	eat a snack
play soccer	watch TV	draw pictures
color pictures	play a game	paint a picture

I like to ___________________

I like to ___________________

I like to ___________________

I like to ___________________

I like to ___________________

I like to ___________________

Flip Fun! Draw a picture showing what you like to do after school.

Summer Words

Name ______________________

sunny
sailing
fishing
swimming
hiking
dry
camping
picnic
bicycling
hot

Find the summer words in the picture. Write them on the lines.

1. ______________________ 6. ______________________

2. ______________________ 7. ______________________

3. ______________________ 8. ______________________

4. ______________________ 9. ______________________

5. ______________________ 10. ______________________

Flip Fun! Draw what you like to do on a hot summer day.

Fairy Tale Fun

Name ______________________

Write the titles of five of your favorite fairy tales.

Word Bank

Beauty and the Beast	The Emperor's New Clothes
Cinderella	The Four Musicians
Goldilocks and the Three Bears	The Gingerbread Boy
Hansel and Gretel	The Little Mermaid
Sleeping Beauty	Three Billy Goats Gruff
Snow White	Three Little Pigs

1. ______________________________

2. ______________________________

3. ______________________________

4. ______________________________

5. ______________________________

Flip Fun! Draw a picture of your favorite fairy tale.

Toys, Toys and More Toys

Name ______________________

Write the names of six toys you would like to have.

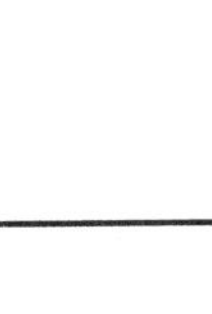

Word Bank

ball	baseball	basketball	bat
blocks	car	clay	computer game
crayons	doll	drum	football
jump rope	marbles	paints	puzzle
soccer ball	top	toy animal	train
bike	truck	kite	skateboard

1. ______________________

2. ______________________

3. ______________________

4. ______________________

5. ______________________

6. ______________________

Flip Fun! Draw a picture of your favorite toy.

Holidays

Name ______________________

Write these holidays in order starting with your favorite.

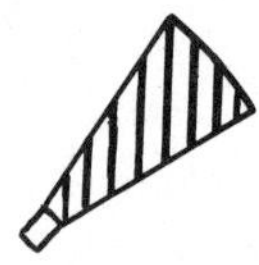
New Year's Day

Valentine's Day

Christmas

Easter

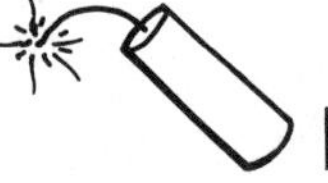
Fourth of July

Halloween

Thanksgiving

1. ______________________

2. ______________________

3. ______________________

4. ______________________

5. ______________________

6. ______________________

7. ______________________

Flip Fun! Draw a picture of your favorite holiday.

What a Way to Travel!

Name ____________________

Write the words in order starting with your favorite way to travel.

1. ____________________
2. ____________________
3. ____________________
4. ____________________
5. ____________________
6. ____________________
7. ____________________
8. ____________________
9. ____________________
10. ____________________

Flip Fun! Draw a picture to show your favorite way to travel.

Write a Rhyme

Name ____________________

Write the titles of the nursery rhymes in alphabetical order.

Jack and Jill
Rain, Rain Go Away
Sing a Song of Sixpence
Hickory, Dickory, Dock
Pease Porridge Hot
Little Bo Peep

1. ____________________

2. ____________________

3. ____________________

4. ____________________

5. ____________________

6. ____________________

Flip Fun! Draw a picture showing your favorite nursery rhyme.

What Day Did You Say?

Name ____________________

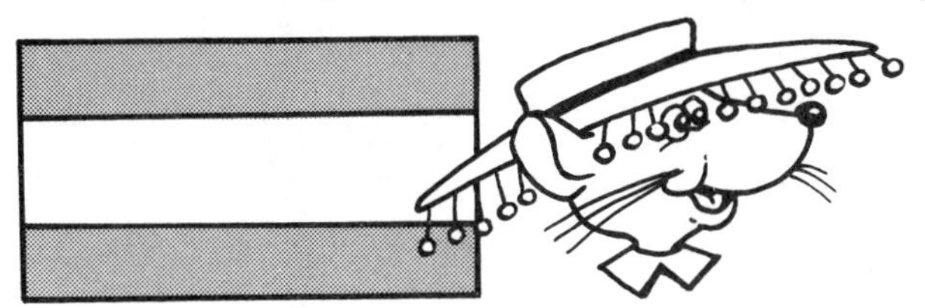

Copy the names of the days of the week in Spanish and in French.

Spanish	English	French
domingo	Sunday	dimanche
lunes	Monday	lundi
martes	Tuesday	mardi
miércoles	Wednesday	mercredi
jueves	Thursday	jeudi
viernes	Friday	vendredi
sábado	Saturday	samedi

Flip Fun! Draw what you like to do on sábado.

Flip Fun! Draw a prize you would like to receive for winning a race.

Far Out!

Name ______________________

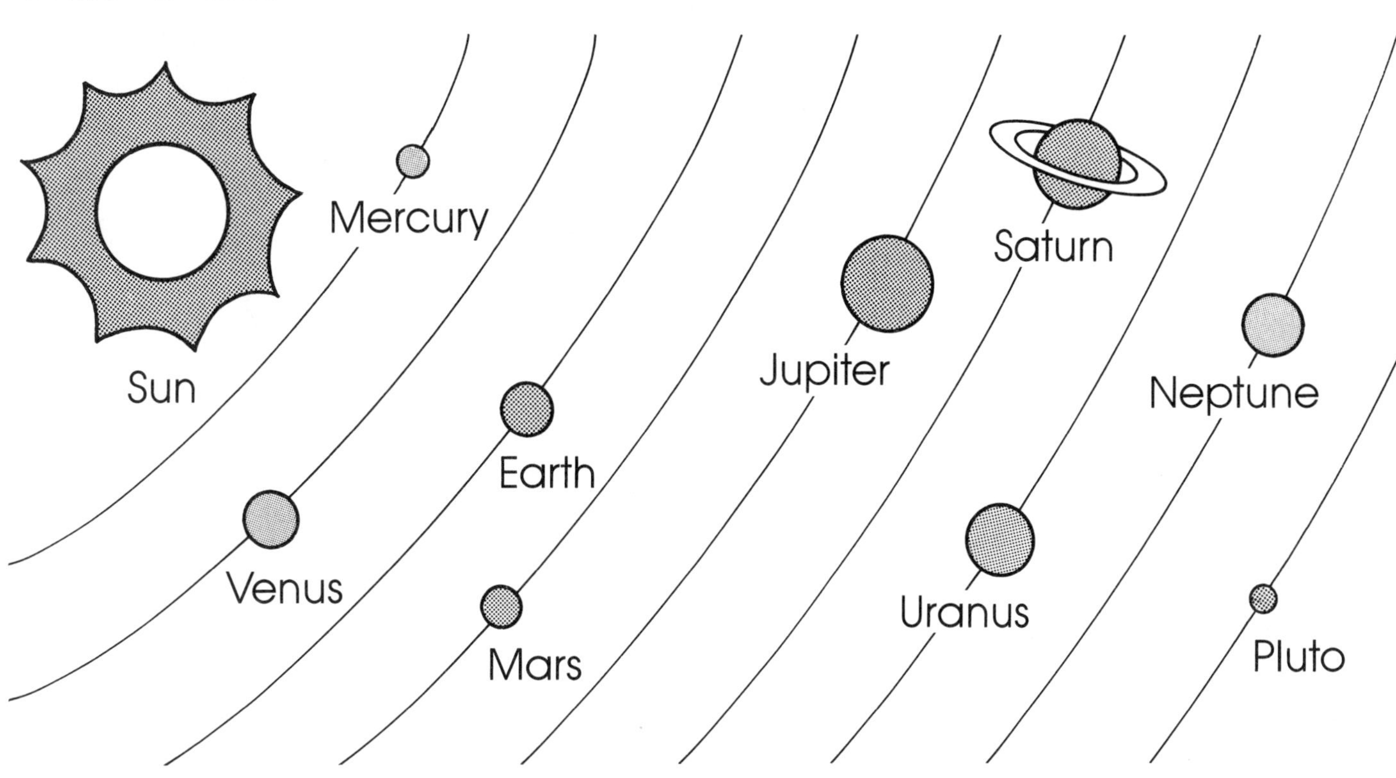

Imagine that you are traveling from the sun to outer space. Write Sun first. Then write the names of the planets in order starting with Mercury.

1. ______________________
2. ______________________
3. ______________________
4. ______________________
5. ______________________
6. ______________________
7. ______________________
8. ______________________
9. ______________________
10. ______________________

Flip Fun! Draw what you think life could be like on another planet.

Attack of the Sweet Tooth

Name ______________________

Write the "sweet treats" in alphabetical order.

Word Bank

pie	doughnut	ice cream	cookie	brownie
milk shake	cupcake	sundae	fudge	cake

1. ______________________
2. ______________________
3. ______________________
4. ______________________
5. ______________________
6. ______________________
7. ______________________
8. ______________________
9. ______________________
10. ______________________

Flip Fun! Draw your favorite "sweet treet."

Countries Around the World

Name ____________________

Write the names of these countries in alphabetical order.

Spain	Germany	Canada	Japan	Australia
Norway	Mexico	United States	France	China

1. ____________________
2. ____________________
3. ____________________
4. ____________________
5. ____________________
6. ____________________
7. ____________________
8. ____________________
9. ____________________
10. ____________________

Flip Fun! Draw a picture of where you would like to go.

Add It Up!

Name ______________________

Add. Write the answer. Then write the number word for the answer.

1	2	3	4	5
one	two	three	four	five

$$\begin{array}{r} 0 \\ +4 \\ \hline \end{array}$$

$$\begin{array}{r} 2 \\ +3 \\ \hline \end{array}$$

$$\begin{array}{r} 2 \\ +2 \\ \hline \end{array}$$

$$\begin{array}{r} 1 \\ +2 \\ \hline \end{array}$$

$$\begin{array}{r} 1 \\ +1 \\ \hline \end{array}$$

$$\begin{array}{r} 1 \\ +4 \\ \hline \end{array}$$

$$\begin{array}{r} 1 \\ +0 \\ \hline \end{array}$$

$$\begin{array}{r} 3 \\ +1 \\ \hline \end{array}$$

Flip Fun! Write five addition problems. Write the answers to the problems.

Add It One More Time!

Name ________________

Add. Write the answer. Then write the number word for the answer.

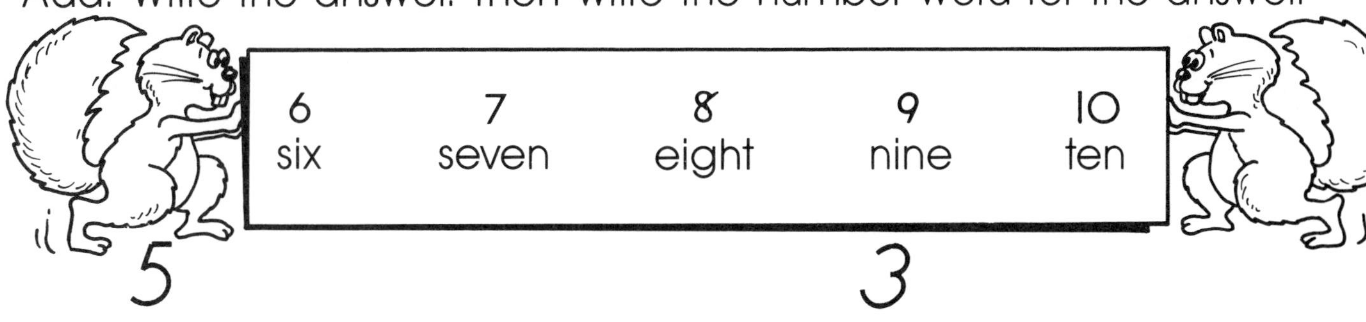

$$5 + 5 = \_\_\_$$ ________________

$$3 + 4 = \_\_\_$$ ________________

$$4 + 2 = \_\_\_$$ ________________

$$8 + 1 = \_\_\_$$ ________________

$$3 + 5 = \_\_\_$$ ________________

$$6 + 4 = \_\_\_$$ ________________

$$1 + 6 = \_\_\_$$ ________________

$$4 + 4 = \_\_\_$$ ________________

Flip Fun! Write five addition problems. Have a friend solve them.

Take It Away!

Name ____________________

Subtract. Write the answer. Then write the number word for the answer.

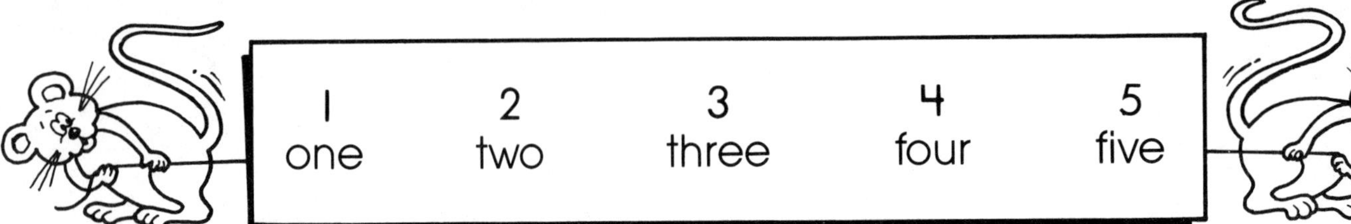

$$\begin{array}{r} 5 \\ -2 \\ \hline \end{array}$$

$$\begin{array}{r} 4 \\ -3 \\ \hline \end{array}$$

$$\begin{array}{r} 4 \\ -2 \\ \hline \end{array}$$

$$\begin{array}{r} 5 \\ -0 \\ \hline \end{array}$$

$$\begin{array}{r} 5 \\ -1 \\ \hline \end{array}$$

$$\begin{array}{r} 4 \\ -1 \\ \hline \end{array}$$

$$\begin{array}{r} 5 \\ -3 \\ \hline \end{array}$$

$$\begin{array}{r} 5 \\ -4 \\ \hline \end{array}$$

Flip Fun! Write five different subtraction problems.

Take Some More Away!

Name ____________________

Subtract. Write the answer. Then write the number word for the answer.

6	7	8	9	10
six	seven	eight	nine	ten

$$\begin{array}{r} 10 \\ -\ 2 \\ \hline \end{array}$$ ______

$$\begin{array}{r} 9 \\ -\ 3 \\ \hline \end{array}$$ ______

$$\begin{array}{r} 8 \\ -\ 1 \\ \hline \end{array}$$ ______

$$\begin{array}{r} 10 \\ -\ 0 \\ \hline \end{array}$$ ______

$$\begin{array}{r} 10 \\ -\ 1 \\ \hline \end{array}$$ ______

$$\begin{array}{r} 8 \\ -\ 2 \\ \hline \end{array}$$ ______

$$\begin{array}{r} 9 \\ -\ 2 \\ \hline \end{array}$$ ______

$$\begin{array}{r} 10 \\ -\ 4 \\ \hline \end{array}$$ ______

Flip Fun! Show 8 – 5 apples.

Antonym Search

Name ____________________

Find the word in the Word Bank to match each picture. Then, draw a line to the word that means the opposite.

Flip Fun! Draw a picture of something hard and something soft.

Get It Together

Name ____________________

Write two words that name things that go together. Write the word **and** between the two words.

Word Bank

bacon	cake	cheese	cookies	crackers	eggs
ice cream	salt	key	lock	milk	pepper
		socks	shoes		

bacon and eggs

Flip Fun! Draw a picture of two things that go together.

Connect the Compounds

Name ____________________

cupcake

Match the two words that go together to make a compound word.

bee	plane
butter	coat
air	hive
rain	fly
bed	noon
after	room

Write the compound words.

1. ____________________

2. ____________________

3. ____________________

4. ____________________

5. ____________________

6. ____________________

Flip Fun! Draw a beehive and five bees.

It Just Makes Sense

Name ____________________

touching

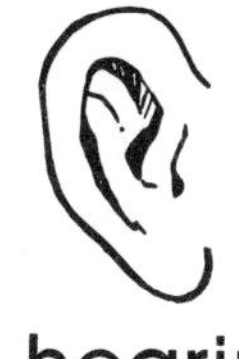
hearing

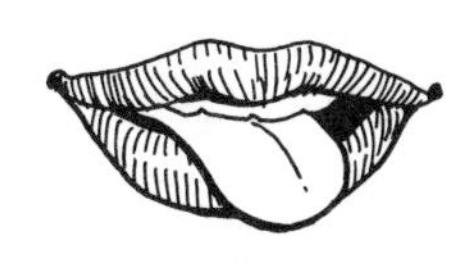
tasting

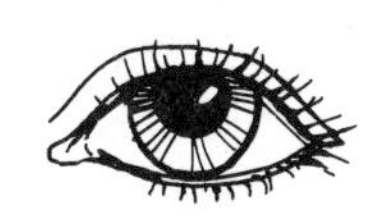
seeing

smelling

Read the words. Write which sense you would use to find out if something is...

1. loud ____________________
2. sweet ____________________
3. burning ____________________
4. yellow ____________________
5. cold ____________________
6. salty ____________________
7. soft ____________________
8. ringing ____________________

Flip Fun! Draw a picture showing something you like to see.

We're Off and Shopping

Name ____________________

Write the words from the Word Bank below the store where the items would be found.

Word Bank

birdcage	bread	cat	dog	drum
flour	hamster	horn	meat	milk
piano	records	sugar	trumpet	turtle

Grocery Store	Pet Store	Music Store

Flip Fun! Draw a picture of a pet you would like to have.

All About School

Name ____________________

Write each of the school words under the correct heading.

Word Bank

crayons	scissors	pencils	boys	girls	glue
handwriting	books	secretary	librarian	math	science
paper	health	social studies	principal	reading	teachers

Classroom Things	Subjects	People

Flip Fun! Draw a picture of your school.

Nouns and Verbs

Name ____________________

Nouns are words that **name** people, places or things. Verbs are **action** words. Write the words where they belong.

Word Bank			
bite	children	donkey	house
jump	kitten	hop	run
school	skip	lunchbox	write

Nouns	Verbs

Flip Fun! Draw a picture of one of the nouns.

Which Direction Should I Go?

Name ______________________

North

West

South

East

Look at the map. Write the missing direction words in the blanks. Then, copy the sentences on the lines.

1. The tree is in the ____________________.

2. There is a swing in the ______________ and ______________.

3. The gate is to the ____________________.

Flip Fun! Draw you and your friend playing in a park.

A Magical Magic Trick

Name ____________________

Unscramble each sentence. Write them correctly on the lines.

1. ____________________________________

2. ____________________________________

3. ____________________________________

Flip Fun! Draw a magic trick that you would like to be able to do.

Barrel Full of Laughs

Name ______________________

1 is a clown. Goofy

2 juggles ten He oranges.

3 inside He rolls barrels.

4 claps. Everyone

Unscramble the sentences. Write them correctly on the lines.

1. ______________________

2. ______________________

3. ______________________

4. ______________________

Flip Fun! Draw a clown doing a silly trick.

Trail Tracks

Name ____________________

Follow the animal tracks to the basket. Write the words in order to make sentences.

1. ____________________

2. ____________________

3. ____________________

Flip Fun! Draw a big rabbit with a carrot.

Put It Together

Name ____________________

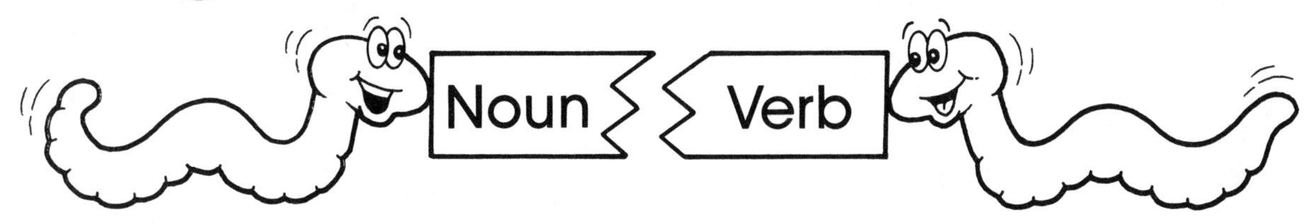

Match the nouns and verbs to make complete sentences. Write the sentences next to the matching pictures.

Nouns	Verbs
A balloon	falls.
The car	pops.
Three bells	speeds.
One apple	eats.
An ape	bakes.
My mom	ring.

1. ____________________

2. ____________________

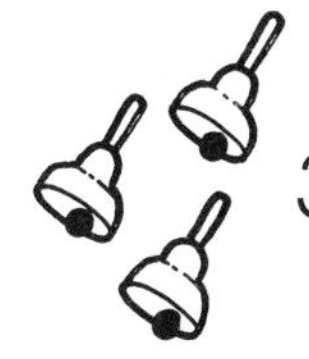

3. ____________________

4. ____________________

5. ____________________

6. ____________________

Flip Fun! Write a sentence of your own. Draw a picture to go with it.

What's Cooking?

Name ______________________

Super Ice-Cream Sundae

2 scoops vanilla ice cream
3 tbls. chocolate syrup
1 squirt whipped cream

Place ice cream in bowl. Pour chocolate syrup over ice cream. Squirt whipped cream on syrup.

Copy the recipe.

Flip Fun! Draw a yummy ice-cream sundae.

Week Days

Name ______________________

Write the sentences correctly with capital letters and question marks where they belong.

Sun.	Mon.	Tues.	Wed.	Thurs.	Fri.	Sat.
picnic	school	movie	museum	park	play	zoo

is sunday or monday the first day of the week

do you watch cartoons on saturday

are we going to see the movie on tuesday or wednesday

Flip Fun! Draw what you like to do on Saturday.

Months

Name ____________________

Write the sentences correctly with capital letters and question marks where they belong.

will it snow in december

how hot does it get in july and august

does school start in september

does your family eat a big feast in november

Flip Fun! Draw a picture of a snow fort you might build.

More Months!

Name ____________

Write the sentences correctly with capital letters and periods where they belong.

kevin and i like to build snow forts in january

summer vacation begins in june

we give cards to our friends in february

i found a four-leaf clover last march

Flip Fun! Draw a beautiful flower garden.

Write Your Own

Name ______________________

The bunny hopped home.

Write your own sentences. Combine words from each list to make complete sentences. Write the sentences on the lines.

List 1	List 2	List 3
Two cars	dropped	the big box.
A tiny bunny	raced	around the track.
They	hopped	high.
He	runs	the ball.
The kitten	swing	into the basket.
We	kicks	after the string.

1. ______________________________

2. ______________________________

3. ______________________________

4. ______________________________

5. ______________________________

6. ______________________________

Flip Fun! Draw a picture of one of the sentences you wrote.

Feelings

Name 

Copy and finish each sentence.

When I feel happy, I...

When I feel sad, I...

When I feel silly, I...

When I feel angry, I...

When I feel scared, I...

When I feel excited, I...

Flip Fun! Draw a picture of you doing something silly.

Color and write.

Name ______________________

My name

My school

My street

My phone

My city

My state

